from blue to you

Janet Huang

BookLeaf Publishing

Presentation by *BookLeaf Publishing*

Web: www.bookleafpub.com

E-mail: info@bookleafpub.com

ISBN: 9789357211734

First edition 2023

DEDICATION

This is for everyone who ever felt lonely, sad and afraid, nursing their wounded hearts, hoping for a better day. You are not alone and you matter.

It's also a book dedicated to all the people who lifted me up, gave me wings, and showed me that it's never too late to live a life that is filled with love and passion.

Without you, none of this would have been possible.

ACKNOWLEDGEMENT

This book could not have been written without the love and support of my family, my big sisters and heroes, Irene and Oradee, Scarborough General Hospital's mental health day program, Bayview Community Services, the YWCA's art therapy program, St Michael's Hospital, and A-Way Express.

Also, all the classical poets who inspired my work (Auden, Tennyson, Thomas, Wordsworth, Poe, Seuss, etc.) and all the awesome instapoets (Atticus, Peppernell, Kaur, etc.)

And finally, for Elizabeth. Words can never convey my gratitude for the great gift you gave me.

PREFACE

A long time ago, in a universe far, far away, there was a humongous dark beast called Depression. It liked to find sensitive souls who were sad because of bad stuff that had happened in their life and suck any joy out of them.

One poor girl was told that she would always be chained to the beast called Depression. She wanted to die. Someone told her it wasn't all bad, that some of the most famous poets and artists had also been so afflicted in the past. So she wrote some very angsty, sometimes bad, yet sometimes very clever rhymes to assuage the Beast. She thought it was a bit melodramatic but she liked it, because it very nicely answered the question of "How are you feeling?" that she never could really answer.

Then she fell in love and someone opened a door that let in all the happy feelings for a while. She felt grateful and alive for the first time in years. She wanted to see and do so many things, to shout out her love to everyone. But love, alas, turns people in to galactic idiots, and she never could find the magic words to make everything better.

So she put this book together, hoping even if it had no easy solutions to offer, that it would help represent the struggles of those who were suffering; that someone might look at these words and relate to them, and thus feel less alone. She also hoped that they might take heart, because it can and does get better.

Flame

The pain I felt was evermore
It hunted joy, it ran ashore
With feet so light, I knew not when
It'd trod its heavy paws again

How canst I rest, when rest is death?
Where doth thou go with thy final breath?
Hell is colder than e'er I knew
And heaven is for the sainted few

You believe in a dream, a dream so pure
That the harshest winds and coldest nights
That batter Your heart, will ne'er know fear
Of the eternal silence or hidden lights

You speak your words, I hear your truth
In golden tones and echoed chimes
I yearn to trust, your words do soothe
My aching soul in tortured times

And yet I rage against the dying of the light
I fight it all with all my might
Is't betrayal, to stoke the flame?
To yearn for more than just the same?

But in the end, when lightning fades
The flame-filled scene is left in shame
The charred reflections an' tattered shades
The silent room, the void remain

A Moment in Time

The rarest flower in the garden
Wilts and soon is gone
A lovely bird sings by itself
A sad and lonely song

Does any soul mourn for my loss
The beauty that was killed?
Does any soul believe my words
That pain was not self-willed?

A moment of time, trembling, still
A memory of light gone by
A reflection of water, shimmering, blue
A tear and a heartfelt sigh

The sun always sets, the gold always fades
Bright colours turn mud as they're swirled
A bittersweet truth, that haunts as it holds
No beauty can stay in this world.

Shadows Fade

Where do you go when the river flows?
Away from darkness and into light
She could not see for the clouds in her mind
She could not be for the pain in her sight

Forever and ever through an aching void
Twisting and turning as if to avoid
A bottomless sorrow, a world with no end
Forever and ever it twisted again

Walking through shadows the chill in her bones
She faded away, she melted in stone
Her voice it did wane as the path disappeared
Her smile was so wan that my eyes they did tear

The wind was a monster it howled through the night
Blew leaves up forever, and swallowed the sound
Of the sob from her lips, as it snuffed out the light
In her eyes as she wavered, all hopes slowly drowned

All alone in her sorrow, outcast in her fear
A solitary shape bent over from shame
Of promises unspoken of trusts she did tear
With a negligent hand she banished all who were near

To hate her forever is what she deserves
To shun her for beauty, to curse her for lies
For unfulfilled words are all that she serves
And to love her is to bleed, as one watches her die

Forever and ever through an aching void
Twisting and turning as if to avoid
A bottomless sorrow, a world with no end
Forever and ever it twists once again.

Colours

Truth is justice
Justice, truth
And nothing in between
Black and white is all there is
So simple and so clean.

Betrayed by the sun
I came much too close
It blinded me before I could see

Now burned in my skull
Is an image in rose
That colours my world for me

Shimmering colours, waver again
No steadiness rests in the world
They capture my brain
They set me aswirl
I pray for it all to end.

Dying forever, lasts a day far too long
Yet living takes more than it gives
O give me your love and I'll promise you this
That something of good will exist.

Hold On

5

I was so lost I could not see
I was so sad I could not be
And in the rivers choices cried
There were no options but to die

Walk softly, never waver in the dust
Stay here until your mind clears
Have faith in better things to come
Remember who you were and trust in love
Strength is in you, remember the calm
You knew who you were for a moment in time
That steadiness rests in you still
Your convictions lie peacefully in your heart
Time passes, just wait, and find yourself still there
Others can never know your truth
The choice is always yours
You can stand your fire just hold true
Hold on, we will get through
Hold on.

Path

There must be a place
Far away from the noise
Where a person can be
Who they are

There must be a time
In between rapid moves
When the heart's free
To heal its scars

Like a path through the reeds
There is always a way
The wind blows a tune
That is true

If we hear with our hearts
What we know will not sway
Then in truth we will know
What to do

Tree

where ever I go
what ever I see
there will always be
a part of me
that remembers your heart
and the bitter black tree

that you understood
though you didn't know me
I see your world and I feel small
though it seems we all must sometimes fall

it hurts sometimes to be alive
when something fine is gone

you are a light, though perhaps you don't see it
you can live in the night, without ever being it

my dreams may be air, but I have known pain
and the things that it does in the dark

it can twist you inside, and blur your self-vision
make you hate who you are, and in this division

some may take their pain, turn it inside out
but we hold it close so it won't get out

instead of hurting others we just hurt ourselves
there must be some middle ground

somewhere beyond
the darkened tree
is a yellow rose
that lives within thee
I can see the gold
and its warmth comforts me

Fight for the gold
For the world
and for me

Integrity

The reality of what you see
Often doesn't mesh
Who you are, and what you be
Can differ in the flesh

But when you find integrity
The world becomes so clear
Honour, grace, and unity
Will encompass every fear

The canvas of reality
Can lift you from the tears
That rend the starry fabric
With the bitterness of years

A dream can be reality
The truth need not be pain
Levity and gravity
Can mix and still give gain

Find whatever makes you whole
Believe and trust again
See the world with eyes anew
Live, and breathe as you.

Blue

How can I describe the cool sweep of blue that flashed
across my view?
As I walked among the sun and breeze, my thoughts rose
up to you
Not far away, but worlds apart, too far away for you?
You saw me as you watched me grow, and wished to see
me through
And I was loved for who I was, by one who saw me true

Shadows dance across your face and time begins to slow
You turn your beauty away from me and suddenly I know
Darkness and light lie in you too, you don't know what to do
And for whatever reasons lurking there, you do not want
me too.

And so I crash in waves and storm, I fall from cliffs so high
My heart so bold, grasps for a hold, as I search for the lie
You do not care, you never did, my past begins to die
You didn't see me as I was, you thought that I could fly

But I remember long ago, a time of green and gold
How much you cared, how young you were, before we both
grew old
I gave my best, was it too much? I never was so true
So in the end, out of my love, I give you back the blue.

Art

How you are right now, is just perfect
You don't have to be anything or do anything
Except what you are in this moment
And it's good. And it's perfect.

Life is painful
But if you take a breath, and look around
You can still see beauty in the little things

Feel the cold air on your face
See the sun's rays light up a tree
Taste the kindness in a cookie
Touch the quiet stillness in a stone
Listen to the voices of people who accept your presence
here
Just the way you are, today

Remember that kindness, wisdom, and love still exist
And that it is stronger than any pain
Your very existence brings us hope
Like a fine piece of art
You shine when you're shared

Feel yourself flow in the swirl of the paint
Let yourself go in the dance of the day
Whisper it in wool, if you feel its soft sway
Pound it all out in the touch of the clay
Choose your own images and words as you may
Make your own music if that's how you play
Shout it all out, if you have something to say
Listen to silence, if that is your way

How you are right now, is just perfect
You don't have to be anything or do anything
Except what you are in this moment

You can go on
It'll be okay

thank you for being part of my day

Asking for Water

Some people
When you ask them for a drink of water
They give you a river
We can only stand in awe (or maybe terror) at their gift

Some people
Without you even having to ask
Will throw you a lifeline
And when a dozen people who are drowning, grab a hold of it
Will somehow pull them *all* safely to shore
We can only stand in awe (or maybe terror) at their gift

Some people
Dive right in the deep end
Without a jacket of their own to help them float
They don't know how deep the tides are
Or the fins within your eyes that won't let go
You think that they are trying to drown you
You try to struggle but they just won't let you go
Until the real sharks circle near you
And make a meal of your former tasty foe
Now their bloated corpse floats near you
As the sharks come close to take a bite
You should let them R.I.P. without you
But it's really hard, for you to let them go
We can only stand in awe (or maybe terror) at their gift

Some people never got the chance to get their feet wet,
While others were wise enough to stay in the shallows
These are the fortunate people who will live
To tell the story, of this watery tale of woe.
Their gift will be to warn others of the dangers
Of trying to save a girl from herself

First Love

Why do I love you?
Nobody knows
You make me want something
To fall apart and melt for you
To let go of all inhibition
To moan, to cry
To find release in your eyes

Your voice is a mystery
So many tones that make me feel
Everything
It reaches to my core
And touches me, places I never knew
I long to give you everything

To stay in your presence
To bask in your warmth
To fly with your laughter
To feel your electrifying touch
To feel comforted by your voice
To marvel at your gracefulness
To fall for your vulnerability
To share your energy
To follow you anywhere
To be with you always

Why do I love you?
Nobody knows
You take away the terror
And bring me joy
New things become possible
Instead of feeling empty
I overflow

Any Time

Love will return
It always does
It's blocked by distance
And by unspoken pain

If I get it out
It will be fine
I really like her
It hurts to be apart

I don't want to hurt
And I need to think
If I feel so strongly again
It will overtake me

She really cared
She really does
I never knew anyone
Who could care so much
Who could want so much
Who could feel so much

And make me feel

I hurt her too
Throughout these months
I didn't know
who I was until I met her
I didn't feel
So strong at first
I still don't know how
To do this

I could just stare at her face
And listen to her voice
And be happy

I just want to be in her presence
For however long it lasts
To make her laugh
To frustrate her
To be teased and feel cared for
To be filled with peace
And joy

To tell her it's okay
to be as she is
To cheer her up
To make her smile
To make her feel
To watch her play
To listen to her forever
To learn all her moods
To hear who she is
To be there for her
when she's feeling sad
To work through the problems
To be her friend
To fill her with thoughts of me
To be her everything

I could feel that way
Any time, she wanted me to
If I ever see her again
If she speaks to me
If she touches me
I will be lost
Unmoored from this windswept rock

Swept away in all that she is
A raging sea of love and lust
I don't know where it ends

When I Die

When I die
I'd like to be the ray of sunshine
That lights your sky
The first green bud of spring
That greets your eye
Your morning cup of coffee
Your innocent smile, when someone sighs
The crackling blaze of warmth, when you want to cry
The gentle wave that washes away your pain
The breeze that cools you on a summer day

When I die
I hope I'll feel the same
That all my love for you, will gather 'round
To bathe your soul in warm contentment
That you may know peace, love, joy, and bliss
While all the pain and all the resentment
All the quiet violence that took place in the shadows
Fades gently in to the night
Gathered in warm arms, to rest, to heal, to sleep
Perchance to dream
Of a better world

Lost Heart

Underneath the bright blue sky,
Lies a child who can not lie
She walks on her hands, without any gloves
Searching for a love, long lost

A sudden clap of lightning
Flashes across the sky
Scaring her witless
Before she can fly

She raises her eyes
She takes a deep breath
But the sun doesn't rise
All she sees is death

A gust of wind lifts up her skirt
A veil of silence descends
The night cloaks a world of hurt
The silence never ends

Up above in the heavens
An angel calls her name
But she is deaf to her cries
And she doesn't feel the same

The rain pours down
Everything falls down
Her heart ever fragile
shatters
At the sound

Her mind wanders here
Her mind wanders there
Searching for the shards
That were lost

Every piece that she finds
Is a puzzle to her
Kind strangers took them in
And grew flowers within

Her heart was so broken!
Now gifted as tokens
To carry other lost ones
To heaven

When they ask for her toll
She has nothing to show
So she walks home
In the snow
Alone

Snowman

I am standing in the shadows
And I know it means nothing
That the people who once loved me
Have been walking out on me

In the village, there's a snowman
Who has never known true warmth
And the carrot that he follows
Never leads him to true north

Every village that he goes to
Every time he calls my name
There's an aching deep inside me
That has never known his name

I am standing here in silence
I am waiting for my turn
There's a million other people
Who would love to see me burn

In the dark I have been followed
In the light I never see
What is right before my senses
What has always followed me

Sun Heart

sun heart
brave heart
holding it all on your own

no one understands
how much
it hurts to be alone

you feel all the colours
and the feelings in the world
they dance for you, they smile at you
they crash, they burn, they swirl

no one understands
because
their eyes, can't see the things you do
their walls are way too high to feel
the feelings that you do

how alone
it is to be
always something wrong
no one would believe you
if you told them weak is strong
but you're the real hero
and I've known it all along
your dream is just as worthy
and I hope to come along

listen
to my heart
as it
sings you
this soft song

sun heart
brave heart
holding it all on your own
you can always
come to me
when you feel
alone

Finding You

Sometimes you know
The proper thing to do
And often that thing
Is to be you

I'm already me!
But is that really true?
There's parts of you
That never shine through

I tried with my heart
To love all that was near
I went up and down
I couldn't see clear

So I tried with my mind
But my mind couldn't find
A path that would mend
A path to the end

A way to reach my heart's desire
Without the whole world complaining
About ice and fire
The end of the world
A change so very dire

So I tried to combine
Both body and mind
But things wouldn't move
The way I wanted them to do

High Heel

Walking through a door
With your pants on fire
Hearing someone tell you
That you're not okay
Feeling the sound of thunder in your veins
As you wander in a land
That's dead and grey

Breathing life in something
That's long been dead
Trying not to laugh
As you hold your head
Crying out in pain
As they count your dead
Feeling something die
Any time we see red

That's the way they dance
On the other side
Sharp and pointy teeth
Will you open wide?
Strip you to your bones
As you try to hide
Memories that they seek
That were deep inside

I have buried something
That was once all mine
Something that was hidden
From another time
It was meant to stay
Somewhere birds don't fly

Now you've gone and opened
What was meant to lie
Come and sing a song
About how hard you try
I will weep with you
When we touch the sky
When the walls fall down
Will we say good bye?

Sloths vs Lions

27

Slow sleepy sloths
Speaking softly
To the sounds
Of silence

Lugubrious lions
Lolling lazily
Like lissome mounds
Of violence

When they wander
Written words are whispered
Winsome rawrs are founded
Violence confounded

All the world watches
With wretched yawns
Writing-- through the ether
Noting naughtily that neither
Wins the war against the weather

When it rains
They both get wet
It doesn't matter why

Follow Your Star

I followed a star
Hoping it would lead me
To where you are

You wiped away my tears
Made me hot cocoa
Blew away my fears

All the time
Denying
You were there

I followed the trail
Left by your breath
In the icy air

You said no to my tale
It was too full of death
And far too unfair

The soldiers didn't hear the order
They marched out of order
They just didn't care
Without you there

The lions didn't leave
They just fell asleep
Peacefully with their sheep

The brooks didn' t run
They dried up in the sun
Like a raisin or a dream
Deferred

Time flew by
While I stood still
Trying to move
Everywhere
Your heart had once
Moved
Me